SCHACHT LAW OFFICE, INC.
2801 Meridian Street
Suite 202
Bellingham, WA 98225

PATENTLY ABSURD

PATENTLY ABSURD

The Most Ridiculous Devices Ever Invented

CHRISTOPHER COOPER

BARNES
&NOBLE
BOOKS
NEW YORK

This edition published by Barnes and Noble Inc.,
by arrangement with PRC Publishing Ltd.

2004 Barnes and Noble Books

10 9 8 7 6 5 4 3 2 1

ISBN 0-7607-5373-3

Produced by PRC Publishing Limited
The Chrysalis Building
Bramley Road, London W10 6SP
An imprint of **Chrysalis** Books Group plc

© 2004 PRC Publishing Limited

Printed in Malaysia

Contents

Introduction

Patents are strange things—even the sanest and most sensible among them (none of which, we hope have strayed into this book) look slightly wacky. A patent forbids anyone to make, or sell, or use some invention except with the permission of the patent-holder. No one may do these things: not even if he or she has developed the invention quite independently of the patent-holder. Ralph Waldo Emerson said that, "If a man can write a better book...or make a better mousetrap than his neighbor, though he build his house in the woods, the world will make a beaten path to his door." Today, before the world could make that proverbial beaten path, you would have to spend a lot of time and a lot of money to find out if someone else has already patented that particular way of snaring the rodents. *Patently Absurd* is a collection of some of the wackiest designs that reach as far back as the early 19th century to the present day and all are illustrated with the original drawings supplied by the inventor.

The United Kingdom claims to have the longest continuous record of

Patents are often used to define everyday objects. Designing a coal-scuttle with a wooden base coated in metal is one of the many useful though obvious ideas to be granted a patent.

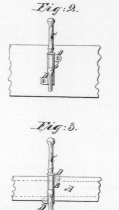

Colburn's design for an improved coat and hat hook was a ridiculously obvious idea thought worthy of a patent.

granting patents. The earliest known was granted by King Henry VI in 1449 to the Flemish-born John of Utynam, who had his own method of making stained glass, giving him a 20-year monopoly.

In the following centuries, the English monarchs busily awarded patents that granted monopolies not only for the sole use of inventions but for the sole right to engage in trades and manufactures in commodities such as soap, leather, glass, and sailcloth. Other governments awarded patents in their own territories and patent laws multiplied. The United States passed its first patent law in 1790, and in 1836 founded the US Patent Office—now the US Patent and Trademark Office (USPTO).

The granting of patents was originally a source of income for the European monarchs. However, there are several respectable reasons for granting patents:

> To ensure a fair reward to an innovator, who might otherwise lose it to an imitator who has not had to bear the costs and labor of developing the invention, or the risks of putting it onto the market.

> To encourage the enterprising to make public the secrets of their innovations. Protected from competition for, typically, several decades, they should have nothing to lose from disclosure.

> To encourage competition. The success in the marketplace of a

patented invention or process encourages others to devise differ-ent—possibly better—ways of achieving the same result, not covered by the patent.

Today mighty fortunes are spent by the large corporations on patents: tracking them down, buying them up, challenging others' patents, defending themselves against challenges to their patents—sometimes even taking out patents on their own innovations.

The great majority of patents cannot be described as weird and wacky: boring and trivial comes closer to the mark. The really screwball minority are the province of the enthusiastic hobbyist or the person who thinks they see a gap in their own trade or indus-try. Certain enthusiasms are perennial and are represented in this collection. They include:

> devices for beautifying the person, male and female, ranging from mus-tache care to dimple creation, from brassieres to derriere slings;
> spherical ships—inventors seem to feel that the rolling oceans require a rolling vehicle;
> devices to get you to sleep and to wake you up;
> devices to embalm you, inter you, or alert the world to the fact that you are not dead;
> countless forms of life-preserver, fire-escape, and general means of escape;
> even more exercise machines than there are diets on the market.

Ways of secreting firearms about the person are also a favorite obsession of the hobby inventor. Not many are in use: it might be that they have proved more lethal to their wear-ers than to the villains they were intended to combat.

Patent examiners are not required to judge whether a hopeful invention is feasible, or useful, or commercially viable; only the test of the marketplace can determine these things. However, patent offices will go so far as to rule out any patent that violates established laws of nature—so you needn't waste your time submitting your perpetual-motion machine to the USPTO. But beyond that, a patent office will confine itself to the task—difficult enough—of finding out whether anything like the proposed invention has already been patented, or whether it is merely an "obvious" application of the already established.

It is often not obvious why an invention is deemed to be not obvious. The improved coat and hat hook of 1864 (US patent 44,853) was an arrangement by which several coat hooks could be slid onto a rail, rather than fastening the hooks directly to the wall. Perhaps its obviousness was overlooked in gratitude for the mastery it gave us over the number and positioning of our coat hooks.

Eighteen sixty-four was a great year for American ingenuity. Thomas T. Markland Jr. suddenly realized that it should be possible (though nothing is completely certain in this life) to perch an iron coal-scuttle on a wooden base instead of an iron one. And if it is objected that a wooden coal-scuttle base is liable to burn when hot ashes fall on it, then why not put a metal cover on it or coat it with "any incombustible material." A grateful nation rewarded him with patent no. 44,875.

These products of the restless mind seem a far cry from the truly earth-shaking creations of great minds, such as Samuel Morse's patent of 1840: nine pages in which he describes his newly invented electric telegraph, the means of generating and recording signals, and the code in which its messages could be sent.

And yet coat hooks and coal-scuttles have played as great a part in the daily lives of most of us as the telegraph and its progeny. Almost every artifact we encounter in our daily lives is, or has been, the subject of a patent. The few score inventors featured in this book are not among those who made our everyday world; but they have enriched it.

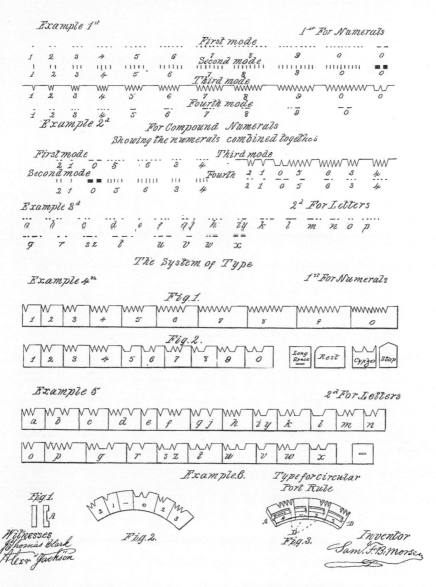

Most patents are useful, though perhaps a little dull, but Morse's idea for an electric telegraph was groundbreaking. His original drawing shows his signature and that of the witnesses.

Improvement in Fire Escapes

Inventor: Benjamin B. Oppenheimer

Date of patent: November 1879 • Patent number: US Patent 221,855

Floating out of the flames

The fortunate user of this invention can step to safety from even the highest story of a burning building. The parachute attached to his helmet brings him gently to earth; the elastic bottom pads of the over-shoes further soften the impact of landing. The inventor's description speaks vaguely of the parachute being "attached, in suitable manner, to the upper part of the body." His artist was bolder: he has shown the user's sole support as being through the helmet's chinstrap. This would probably have given the aeronaut such a wrench that he would have arrived at the ground with a broken neck.

Device for Assisting Infirm Persons

Inventor: A. Eustis

Date of patent: March 1895 • Patent number: US Patent 535, 825

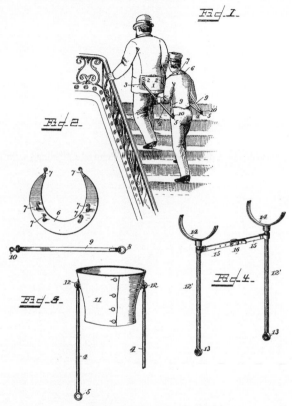

Bellboy not included

This device was proposed to help the infirm but affluent to climb stairs. Doubtless those for whom it was intended were grateful that the widespread adoption of the elevator soon made it unnecessary. It consists (*Figure 1*) of a pressure plate pushed against the assisted person's lumbar regions by a vigorous young hotel employee or other servant. This assistant wears a yoke, or collar (*Figure 2*), to which are attached the swiveling rods that are joined to the pressure plate. Figure 3 shows a waistband that could replace the pressure plate. Figure 4 shows yet another alternative—stirrup-shaped supports that could be positioned in the beneficiary's armpits.

Cigarette Holder Ring

Inventor: Paul R. Johnston

Date of patent: January 1976 • Patent number: US Patent 3,930,510

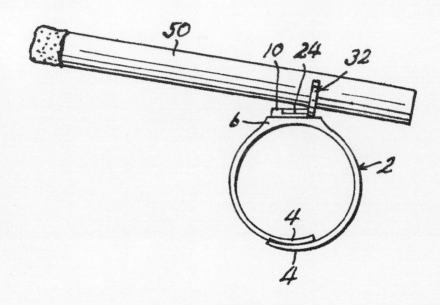

Smoke ring

The long cigarette-holders used by vamps and lounge lizards of the 1920s had an undeniable glamour, but they were not in evidence by the 1970s. Whatever the reason for their loss of popularity, this inventor thought that something was needed for those who want to keep their hands free at moments when their cigarettes are not actually in their mouths. This cigarette holder ring is fitted with a clip that is folded away in the crown of the ring when not in use. When it is brought into play, it can be turned to any angle. This invention would certainly keep the cigarette out of the way; but might it also keep it out of mind, with disastrous consequences if the user were to shake hands with someone?

Exercising Device

Inventor: C. G. Purdy

Date of patent: August 1923 • Patent number: US Patent 1,466,559

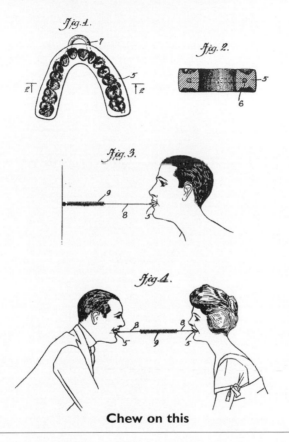

Chew on this

If more people worried about whether their teeth were getting all the exercise they require, this device might be as common as the exercise bicycle. It consists of a plate shaped to the bite of the person for whom it is made and is gripped in the mouth. One end of a cord is attached to the front of the plate and the other end to a spring. One person can exercise solo (*Figure 3*), moving his head back and forth to apply gentle rhythmic stress to the teeth and gums. But two can enjoy a dental workout (*Figure 4*) while gazing into each other's eyes. However, it would be inadvisable for either partner to open his or her mouth to suggest that it's time to stop.

Apparatus for Obtaining Criminal Confessions

Inventor: Helene Adelaide Shelby

Date of patent: March 1930 • Patent number: US Patent 1,749,090

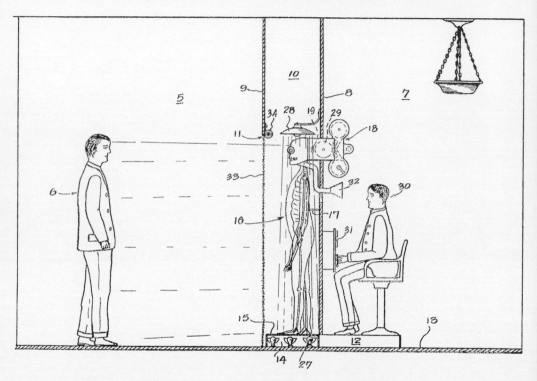

Bringing out that skeleton in the closet

The key feature of this Californian patent is not the concealed camera and sound-recording equipment for permanently preserving a suspect's confession and his "every expression and emotion." No, the real genius is the figure in the form of a skeleton, "an apparatus for the creation of illusory effects calculated to impress the subject with their being of a supernatural character and to so work upon his imagination as to enable an inquisitor operating in conjunction with the recording system to obtain confessions." It might not only have been the superstitious criminal with whom this would have been effective; a bout of uncontrollable hilarity might relax any criminal sufficiently to confess.

Device for Waking Persons from Sleep

Inventor: Samuel S. Applegate

Date of patent: April 1882 • Patent number: US Patent 256,265

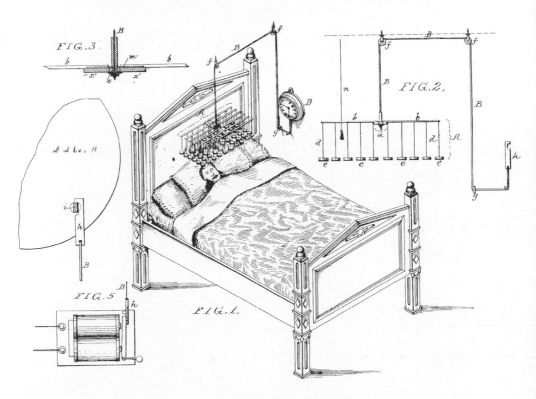

In your face

As this inventor points out, "ordinary bell or rattle alarms are not effective for their intended purpose, as a person in time becomes so accustomed to the noise that sleep is not disturbed when the alarm is sounded." So this frame is suspended over the sleeper's head and released by a clock at the appropriate time in the morning. Hanging from the frame are a number of cords carrying balls of cork or other light objects, "the only necessity to be observed in constructing the frame being that when it falls it will strike a light blow...not heavy enough to cause pain." In addition, while the newly-awakened person lies there, battered and wishing that the snooze button had been invented, the device automatically lights a gas lamp.

Device for Producing Dimples

Inventor: Martin Goetze

Date of patent: May 1896 • Patent number: US Patent 560,351

The dimple made simple

The inventor—"a subject of the King of Prussia"—explains that his apparatus will either produce dimples or nurture and maintain dimples already existing. There is a small changeable massage knob (c) at the lower end, which is placed at the selected place. Rotating the device causes the small revolving massage-cylinder, (f) to "mass and make the skin surrounding the spot where the dimple is to be produced malleable." Such a massaging effect is necessary, the inventor claims, to make the body susceptible to the production of "artistic dimples."

Apparatus for Signaling from Graves

Inventors: E. S. Crosby and E. R. Henry

Date of patent: August 1904 • Patent number: US Patent 766,171

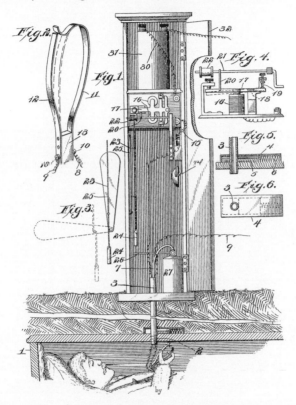

The air-conditioned grave

Such was the reputation of the medical profession at the time that our forebears had a morbid fear of being prematurely buried. Devices abounded to signal the mistake to those above. In this one, an electric switch (*Figure 2*) is placed in the hand of the presumed deceased before the casket is closed. Should he revive, a very slight pressure on the switch completes an electric circuit. An electric bell (*14*) sounds; a signal goes along a wire (*9*) and sounds another alarm at the house of the sexton; a signal arm (*3*) is raised; and a supply of oxygen (*27*) is switched on to sustain the unwilling resident of the grave until help arrives. As it turned out, nobody was dying to use it.

Saluting Device

Inventor: J. C. Boyle

Date of patent: March 1896 • Patent number: US Patent 556,248

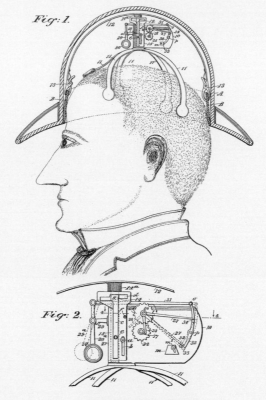

A real head-turner

Gentlemen hate having to put their bags and parcels down to doff their hats to ladies they meet; or they did in the days when gentlemen wore hats and ladies expected to have them doffed. This device stream-lined the process with technical wizardry that could be relied on to gain the fascinated attention of any lady greeted in this way. Merely bowing would cause the spring-driven mechanism gently clamped to the head to raise the hat a small distance, rotate it once and replace it; thereby, in the words of the inventor, "effecting a polite salutation without the use of the hands in any manner."

Animal-Powered Drive

Inventor: P. A. Barnes

Date of patent application: April 1981 • Patent number: British Patent GB2060081

Fig.2.

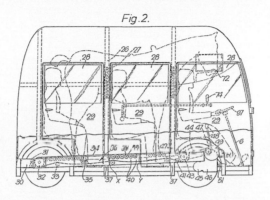

Fig.4.

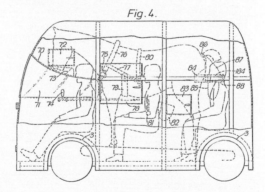

The horse-bus

Even the most environmentally conscious travelers would probably not relish returning to the horse-and-cart as a means of transport. This invention would combine the benefits of modern vehicle design with the charm of horse-drawn transport. The horse walks on an endless belt, which powers the rear wheels. The driver controls the vehicle with a steering-wheel, clutch, and gearbox. Passengers have a smooth, if slow, ride as they sit in comfort alongside the horse, which mercifully is fitted with a bag to collect droppings. The machine is doubly environmentally friendly in that it would never travel fast enough to produce any roadkill, not even a sauntering snail.

Bird Diaper

Inventor: Lorraine Moore and Mark Moore

Date of patent: August 1999 • Patent number: US Patent 5,934,226

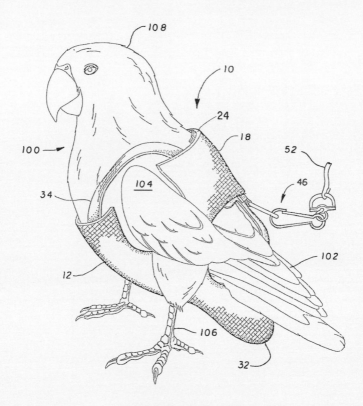

Flight without fear

Many families have pet birds that they love dearly and that they love to have roaming freely round the house. But they often have furniture that they love equally dearly, not to mention exposed food, babies' cots and so on; and birds can rarely be house-trained. Here is the solution: a diaper, tailored to the size of the bird, allowing free movement to the wings and having a hole for the tail. In use, the bird will scarcely notice it—though the fact that the upper part of the diaper seems to be holding down the bird's flight feathers might restrict it to a small glide—but the human beings around the place will be grateful for it.

Eating Appliance

Inventor: Jean B. A. La Jeunesse

Date of patent: March 1922 • Patent number: US Patent 1,409,731

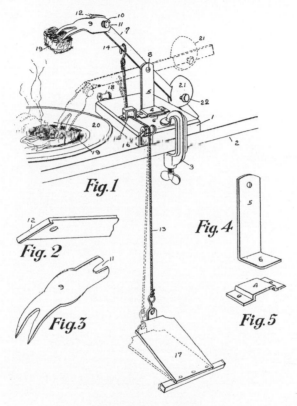

Fig. 1

Fig. 2

Fig. 3

Fig. 4

Fig. 5

Automatic eater

This device was intended to assist the disabled who have difficulty in lifting food to their mouths. A swiveling arm was held upright by a weight (*21*). The user could bring the arm down by means of the pedal (*17*), and the fork on the end would spear a portion of food on the plate. The whole device could be fixed to the table by means of a G-clamp and removed when it was no longer needed. And the device has an additional pulley (*18*) to be used if the device is needed by a left-handed person. The words simple and effective... don't come to mind.

Floor-Polisher

Inventor: Lili Aline McGrath

Date of patent: April 1915 • Patent number: US Patent 1,136,150

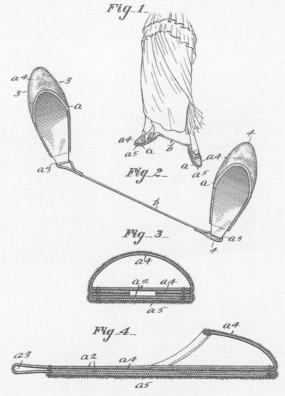

Slipping and sliding

This boon to the homemaker consists of a pair of over-slippers, the soles of which are of a material suitable for polishing the floor in question. They are joined by a cord sufficiently long to permit a full stride of the wearer, but not long enough to permit the legs to spread so far as to cause a fall. The inventor, waxing lyrical in her application, mentions that the wearer "begins to dance, preferably such dances as require long glides, and it will be seen that the floor-polishing operation becomes a pleasure and, also, the entire weight of the wearer is utilized instead of merely the weight of the upper part of the body…"

Swimming Apparatus

Inventor: W. Beeson

Date of patent: July 1881 • Patent number: US Patent 243,834

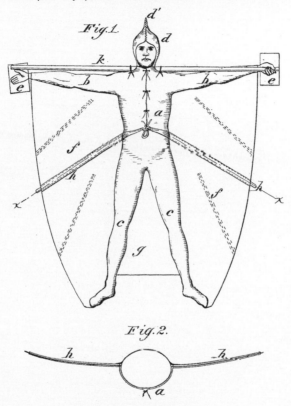

Underwater flying

This swimsuit is presumably intended to make swimming faster and easier, although the purpose of this "novel swimming apparatus" is never fully explained. It consists of a suit "provided with pockets or receptacles for the body and limbs," and wings extending between the wrists and the feet. Struts (*h*) prevent the wings from folding up in use. The crossbar (*e*) provides support for the hands and arms of the wearer. The inventor is remarkably confident about the powers of his device: he says blithely: "If found desirable…the same principle and structure may be employed for flying through the air." Someone who clearly wrote his patent before he tried it out.

Baby-Patting Machine

Inventor: Thomas V. Zelenka

Date of patent: January 1971 • Patent number: US Patent 3,552,388

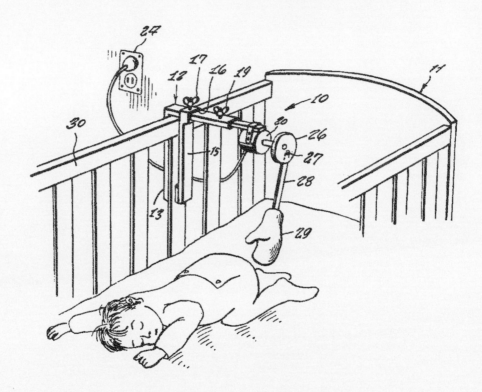

The patter of a tiny seat

It's not known how many exhausted parents were brought respite by this machine. The idea is to get Junior off to sleep by patting his or her rump gently and repeatedly with the aid of some simple technology. The rotary motion of the electric motor mounted on the side of the crib is converted into a back-and-forth motion of the arm carrying the soft mitt. Presumably this worked well in Mr. Zelenka's family with children glued into one place; but it's hard to believe he didn't account for babies turning round or moving off. The same device used today would probably lead to a minor conviction.

Dust Cover for Dog

Inventor: Seroun Kesh

Date of patent: September 1964 • Patent number: US Patent 3,150,641

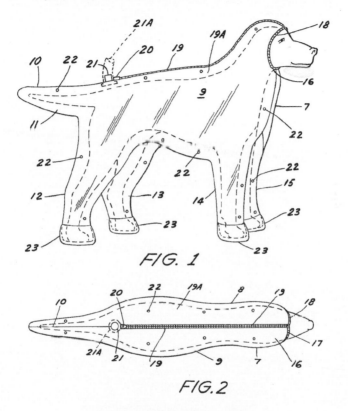

FIG. 1

FIG. 2

One small step for a dog...

No, it's not a space-suit for a dog, or a cover to keep the groomed mutt pristine before it goes to the show: its job is to keep newly applied anti-pest powder or spray on the pet, and away from everyone and everything else in the house. The dog is placed in the plastic coverall by means of the zipper (*19*). The built-in boots prevent it from scratching and damaging the garment. Ventilation holes (*22*) keep the occupant comfortable. Equally usefully, the garment can be used as a drying suit after a bath: connect a hair-dryer to the inlet (*21*), and the pooch will soon be warm and dry. Of course, a suitably sized and shaped suit could be used for your cat (anti-scratch gauntlets extra).

Automated Bathing Facility

Inventor: Gyda Hallum

Date of patent: December 1969 • Patent number: US Patent 3,483,572

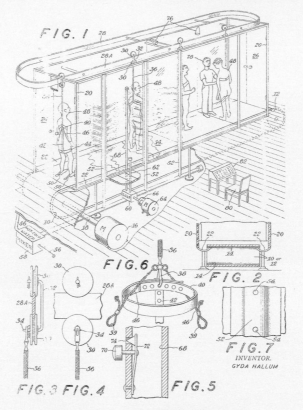

We have ways of getting you clean

Patients in mental institutions or homes for the elderly are sometimes resistant to being bathed. This facility will deal with even the most willful. The "clients," supported by straps hanging from an overhead rail, stand on a conveyor belt to which their feet are securely strapped. They are transported without further effort on their part through a series of stations for wetting, soaping, rinsing, and drying by infrared lamps or hot air. No need for attendants, wash-cloths, and towels. Hey, with a little modification, the same principle could be used to give them their meals and walk them in the gardens...

Head-Mounted Double-Motor-Driven Toy

Inventor: John Yeh

Date of patent: March 1988 • Patent number: US Patent 4,729,747

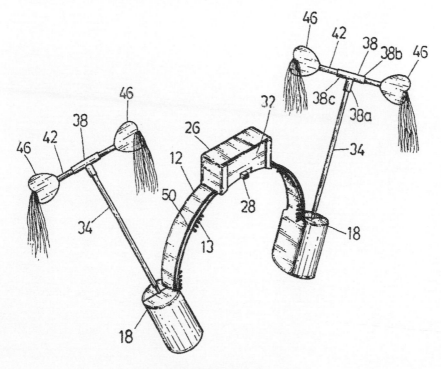

For the well-balanced child

"The present invention," states the application, "may be preferably but not necessarily mounted on top of a child's head." It's difficult to imagine where else it might be used. It consists of a headband carrying two "rotating attractive articles," powered by batteries. The leap forward consists in the fact that the working parts with their motors are two in number, balanced and low on the head, marking an end to the lop-sidedness that has spoiled the enjoyment of past generations of head-toy-wearing children.

Mouth-Closing Device

Inventor: Richard Garvey

Date of patent: September 1930 • Patent number: US Patent 1,775,718

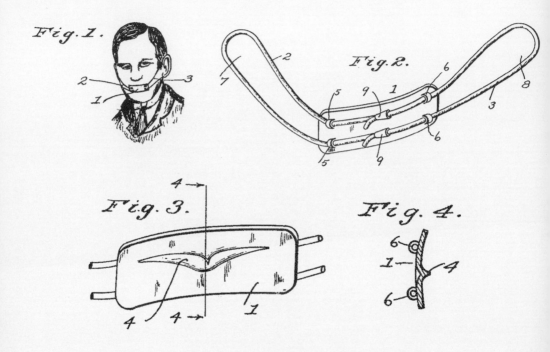

Close secret

Sometimes it's wise to keep one's mouth closed; perhaps the doctor recommends breathing through the nose, or perhaps one snores at night. This invention claims to close your mouth, or rather, to cover the mouth so that the wearer cannot breathe through it. It consists of a pad of suitable material, a shaped protuberance that fits between the lips in order to prevent it from slipping up or down, and adjustable loops to fit over the ears. The user shown seems to be dressed for the office; perhaps the mouth-closer is the only way he can be sure of not saying anything rude to the boss.

Scratching and Petting Device for Pets

Inventor: Rita A. Della Vecchia

Date of patent: October 1989 • Patent number: US Patent 4,872,422

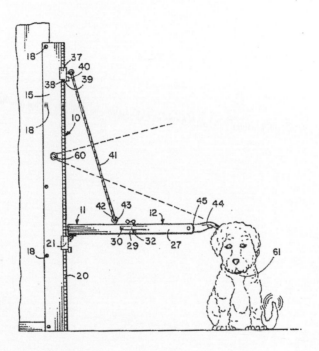

A master stroke

Pets that demand to be stroked and petted can be a little wearying after a while. With this device they would be able to be fondled whenever they chose, which in the case of a dog would probably be whenever it wasn't being fed or walked. The horizontal arm can be mounted higher or lower, according to the size of the pet. The arm is jointed in the middle, and the outer part is swung horizontally from side to side, being automatically activated by an infrared sensor eye. (This device is soon to be followed by one that throws sticks.)

Steam or Hot Air Apparatus

Inventor: Richard Mayer

Date of patent: January 1910 • Patent number: US Patent 945,241

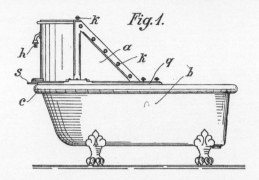

Fig. 1.

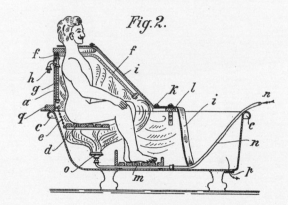

Fig. 2.

A hot idea

This hood will fit over an ordinary bathtub to turn it into an instant steam-bath. The seat is attached to the hood, so your body weight pulls the hood down tightly, making a close seal to retain the heat. Now all you need is a supply of steam via the pipe at the right. Your butler will have to leave his other duties while he operates the supply.

Hammock Canoe

Inventor: Edward H. Brown

Date of patent: June 1884 • Patent number: US Patent 299,951

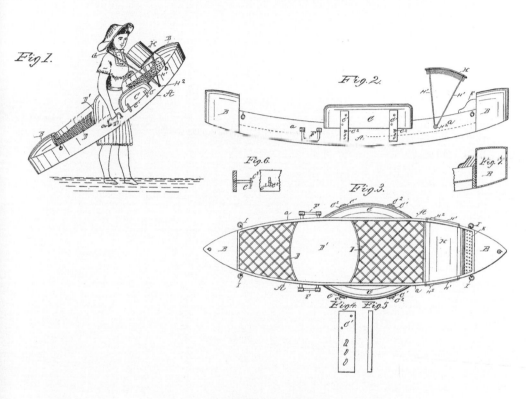

Swing 'n' float

Here's a boat that you can actually wear as you carry it into the water, thanks to the aperture in the open-mesh floor. The air chambers (*B*) and (*C*) ensure that the device actually floats. After all that lugging you'll need a rest, so you can float lazily around in the shallows for an hour or two. (Note the built-in awning *H*, and inflatable pillow, *K*.) Then you can take the canoe home, hang it up and—now needing to recover after the trip—use it as a hammock. The inventor doesn't mention it, but the hole in the middle looks like the handiest way yet devised to get into or out of a hammock without rolling off.

Life Raft

Inventor: Henry Robert Rowlands

Date of patent: December 1858 • Patent number: US Patent 22,457

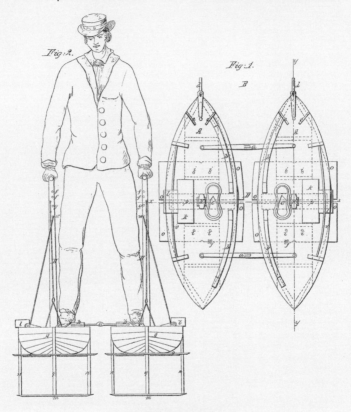

Sea strollers

This invention is subtitled "Apparatus for Walking on the Water," but perhaps the inventor decided that "Life Raft" was a less messianic-sounding main title. The sailor, escaping from his sinking ship or perhaps just going ashore on leave, stands on twin boats, held together by two swiveling bars (*a*). Steadying himself with the stanchions, or upright poles (*H*), he moves each foot forward in turn, just as in walking. Hinged flaps beneath the boats permit them to move forward easily, but resist backward motion. The boats have movable pieces of iron for ballast, as well as rudders and even small pumps to remove water. If Mr. Rowlands had made them a little larger and added seats and oars, he would have invented the lifeboat.

Protecting Armor for Cycle Riders

Inventor: Frank Marcovsky

Date of patent: June 1915 • Patent number: US Patent 1,144,150

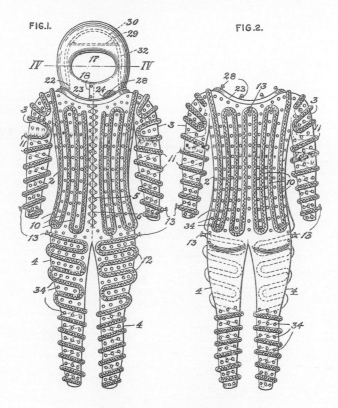

Take me to your leader

This armor for riders of cycles, either pedal or motor, was proposed when war was raging in Europe. But this wasn't bulletproof armor for the battlefield: it was inflatable armor for protection on the highways of America. Tubes, inflatable with an ordinary bicycle pump, spiral around the outside of the torso, arms, and legs of a one-piece suit. The helmet consists of an inner and outer part, the space between them forming an inflatable air cushion. Wearing this suit, a rider caught in a crash could bounce to safety. The tubes were protected by tough coverings, so fixing a puncture in the suit could be quite a challenge.

Airplane of Rooster Shape

Inventor: Angel Mateo

Date of patent: June 1931 • Patent number: US Patent 1,810,182

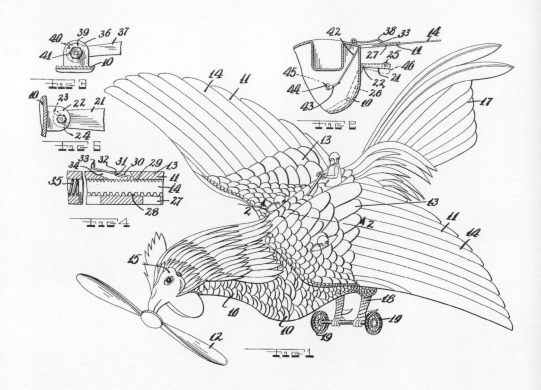

Feather-brained

Now why would anyone want to fly in an airplane that looks like a rooster? Well, you can read right through Mr Mateo's patent application and be none the wiser, because he doesn't give a single reason why he wants his "aeroplane" (the word he uses) to be like that. Perhaps he thought he could make a fortune using it to advertise fried chicken or stock cubes. Anyway, as rooster-style planes go, Mr. Mateo reckons it's a great advance. For one thing, it has flapping wings. Unfortunately, such ornithopters, as they're called, have never been a success, and the rooster plane continues that great tradition.

Comb-Mounted Hair Analysis Gauge

Inventor: Ray Wilson

Date of patent: August 1969 • Patent number: US Patent 3,459,197

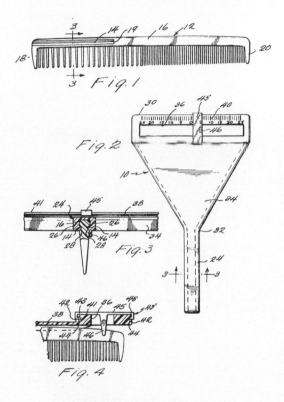

A-head of its time

Many disorders threaten the hair, explains this inventor: "thinning, kinking, drying, becoming oily, becoming damaged from bleach or other chemicals…presence of expended hair care and styling preparations such as hair spray." But "barbers, beauticians, hair and scalp specialists" can monitor the condition of your hair by using this device to see how hard it is to drag a comb through it. As the comb flexes when used, it pushes a slider (45) along the fixed scale (40). The scale ranges from zero deflection (you've gone bald) to maximum (comb snaps—you definitely need to wash that hair).

Churn in Rocking Chair

Inventor: Alfred Clark

Date of patent: January 1913 • Patent number: US Patent 1,051,684

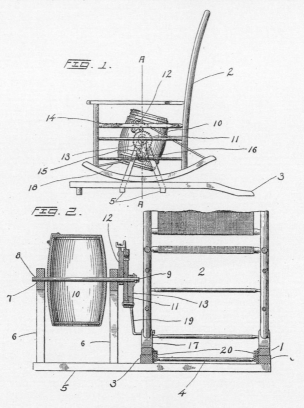

This one rocks

When grandpa gets too old to milk the cows, there's no reason why he shouldn't continue to do his bit on the farm. While he's rocking the hours away, his chair can be hooked up to this butter churn. Of course, he'll complain that rocking is hard work nowadays, since he has to move the churn as well as himself; but he always did complain a lot, and anyway, the exercise will do him good. No dozing off, now, Gramps… that butter has to get to market…

Combined Plow and Gun

Inventors: C. M. French and W. H. Fancher

Date of patent: June 1862 • Patent number: US Patent 35,600

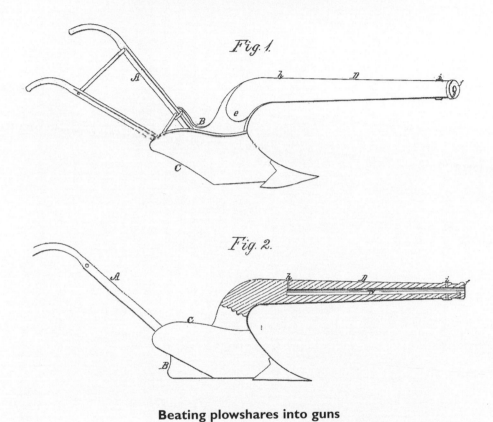

Fig. 1.

Fig. 2.

Beating plowshares into guns

Strongly evocative of the desperate struggle going on at the time it was proposed, this "new and improved ordnance plow" could offer quick resistance to "surprises and skirmishing attacks on those engaged in a peaceful avocation." It could be quickly loosened from the team pulling it and swung into position with the plow-handles. The blade of the plowshare would anchor it in the ground to resist the recoil of the shot. The inventors claimed the gun could be made large enough to fire a ball of one to three pounds weight without hindering the plowing. But be careful not to shoot your own cows or horses.

Combustible Gas-Powered Pogo Stick

Inventor: Gordon Spitzmesser

Date of patent: January 1958 • Patent number: US Patent 2,929,459

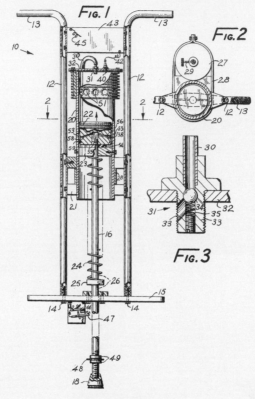

Jump on the gas

To a nervous parent, even an ordinary pogo stick can seem a little dangerous for a child; but take heart—it could be a lot more dangerous, as this invention shows. This motorized pogo stick, "for use by children and adults alike," contains a gasoline engine that fires every time the bottom of the stick hits the ground. What heights little Johnny might reach, the patent application does not speculate. What is certain is that he would regale the neighbors with a noise like a cross between a motor-mower and an air-hammer. The application promises that the motorized pogo stick will be "of tremendous entertainment value"—for the sort of spectator who slows down to look at highway accidents.

Combination Hunter-Fisher Survival Unit

Inventor: James F. White

Date of patent: October 1964 • Patent number: US Patent 3,154,063

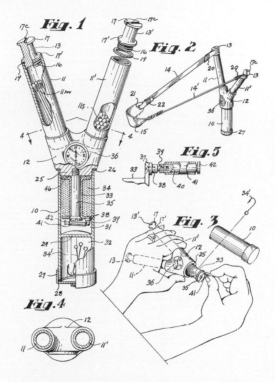

For the boy scout who has everything

Here's a combined gadget for hunting, fishing, and general camping uses. It has the overall form of the classic slingshot, but it's hollow, and inside are matches and buckshot, a reel, line, and hooks for fishing. The inventor says, "I have experienced the time and place, behind the enemy lines in World War II, when this unit would have provided us with fresh meat and fish and greatly added to our iron rations and our well being." And, of course, there's a built-in compass to help you find your way to the mall when all else fails.

Shark Protector Suit

Inventors: Nelson C. Fox and Rosetta H. V. G. Fox

Date of patent: May 1989 • Patent number: US Patent 4,833,729

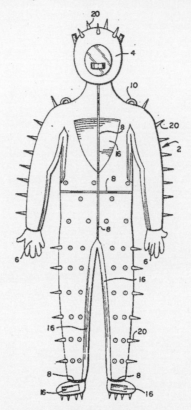

Go ahead, shark—make my day

"The suit and helmet have a plurality of spikes extending outward therefrom to prevent a shark from clamping its jaws over the wearer." Not only a plurality of spikes, but a plurality of metal plates are inserted in the suit, in the most vulnerable areas of the wearer, the chest, inner legs, and seat. A plurality of zippers festoon the suit to help the wearer take it off and put it on. No danger there; it's well known that sharks can't work zippers. With all this protection, and all the trouble they've gone to just to put it on, a diver might well be tempted to go and pick a fight with a shark.

Firearm Mounted in a Shoe Heel

Inventor: Fred E. Stuart, Sr.

Date of patent: January 1971 • Patent number: US Patent 3,557,481

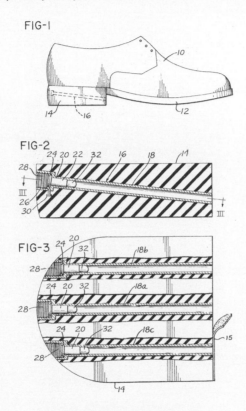

FIG-1

FIG-2

FIG-3

The weapon of a heel

In case this invention seems a little alarming, take comfort from the assurance that only "military personnel and police and other authorized persons" would be allowed this fearsome footwear. Bullets would be loaded from the rear into the barrels set in the heel. A very strong impact of the heel on a hard surface, with the foot raised to the firing angle, would discharge the bullet in the general direction of a criminal. The application assures us that ordinary pressure and impact couldn't set the shoe-gun off. And if by chance the shoe-gun did fire accidentally, the bullet, being at the wrong angle, would merely bounce off the ground and blow the wearer's foot off. Not one for tap-dancing law enforcement officers.

Birthday Cake Candle Extinguisher

Inventor: Paul Bosak

Date of patent: September 1964 • Patent number: US Patent 3,150,831

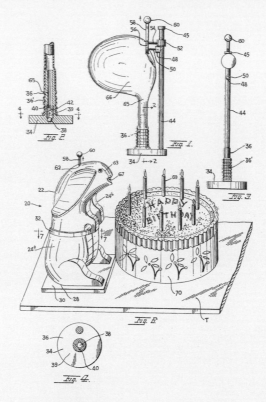

No frothing over the frosting

Why is the cute toy monster sitting next to the birthday cake? Because inside it is an inflated balloon, which can be popped by a needle operated from outside. This causes a puff of air to come from the mouth, blowing out the candles. As Mr. Bosak says, "This device fulfills a long-felt need at birthday parties for small children who may have insufficiently forceful breath to extinguish candles on a cake." Even more importantly for many a parent with grim memories of birthday-cake enthusiasm, it "avoids the unsanitary condition encountered when children inexpertly blow on candles and inadvertently expectorate upon the cake."

Amphibious Motorcycle

Inventor: S. Du Bose

Date of patent: November 1974 • Patent number: US 3,848,560

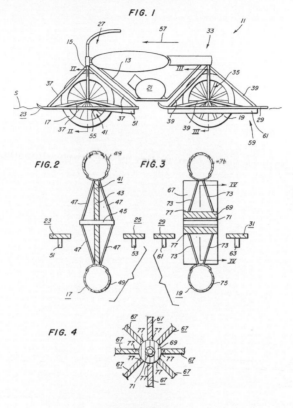

Wet biking

Ever felt tempted to drive a motorbike into a lake to see what happens? Not altogether an unheard of possibility with this invention, an adaptable motorbike that handily converts into a waterborne vehicle by means of skis. The "forward and rearward skis keep the motorcycle waterborne so long as the motorcycle is suitably propelled," says the inventor, ominously. If the engine cuts out in the middle of the lake, the rider is sunk—literally. A wetsuit and a proficiency in swimming are recommended.

Combined Racing Greyhound Harness and Rider Supporting Means

Inventor: Rennie Renfro

Date of patent: September 1933 • Patent number: US Patent 1,926,420

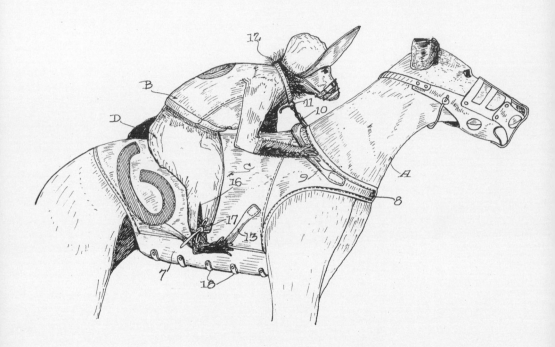

All this, and he has to work for peanuts

"In the sport of greyhound racing there has been recently introduced the use of monkey riders…the monkey jockey adds considerable zest and enjoyment to the sport," says this inventor. "To assure against accidental displacement of the jockey, I have devised the present combined harness and rider support." The secret is that the monkey is attached to the greyhound's harness by all four paws and by the neck. To make assurance doubly sure, its pants are sewn to the dog's harness. Doubtless the monkey is grateful for this concern for its comfort and safety, but it must be tough to get out of the gear to collect the trophy when it wins.

Life Saving Apparatus

Inventor: Michael Kispéter

Date of patent: June 1915 • Patent number: US Patent 1,143,835

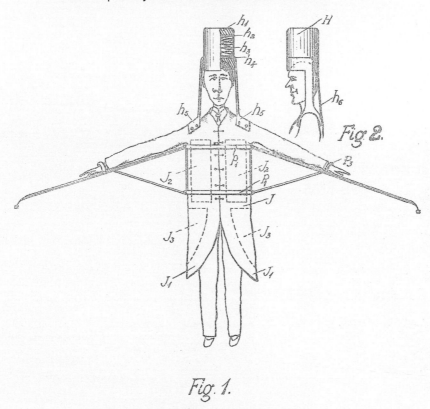

Fig. 1.

The well-dressed aeronaut

It would take a full demonstration by the cabin crew to properly explain this multi-component "life-saving apparatus for aeronauts." A rather snappy coat has built-in air cushions to keep you up if you fall into water. A parachute is worn over the coat, essentially a circle of fabric that is supported by hinged rods. If you should fall on land, your head will be protected from injury by a metal crash-helmet, supported on your shoulders. It also has a spring-loaded top to absorb the shock, or to keep you bouncing. The safety device was not adopted by commercial airlines who would have needed a seat the size of a sofa to fit it underneath.

Improvement in Road Lanterns

Inventor: Lorenzo G. Macauley

Date of patent: April 1879 • Patent number: US Patent 214,422

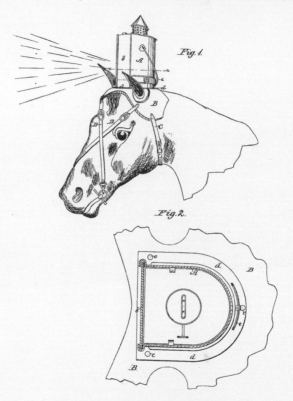

Dobbin gets light-headed

This lantern is held securely to the horse's hood by means of metal rivets, and is easily detached. The inventor says, "A lantern thus attached to a horse's head enables both horse and driver to see the condition of the track and the objects in it much more plainly and at a greater distance than when a lantern is placed on the carriage." Though not so well as when worn on the driver's head, perhaps. It would certainly need a well disciplined steed: any tossing of the head, or looking to left or right, would defeat the object of the device. Would the horse have been trained to dip the light for oncoming traffic...?

Derriere Exerciser

Inventor: Ahmet M. Ozbey

Date of patent: April 1982 • Patent number: US Patent 4,325,379

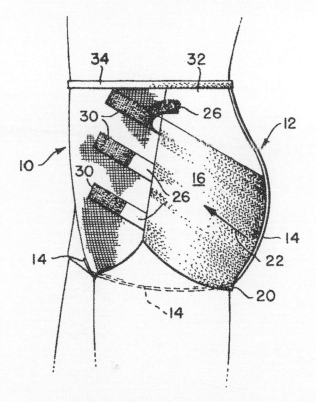

A beautiful butt without tears

The inventor explains that formerly "it has been necessary for a person desiring to improve his or her muscle tone in the buttocks or pelvic floor area to consciously perform a series of exercises for this purpose." That dark age is past. The present invention separates the buttocks by means of the strip (*14*) and lifts them by means of the panels (*16* and *18*) into an "unnatural" position by means of the crossed bands. The muscles try to assume their natural position, resulting in automatic isometric exercise, of which the wearer is unconscious. Just the sort of exercise we all like.

Liquid Brassiere

Inventor: James O. Moreau

Date of patent: March 1988 • Patent number: US Patent 4,734,078

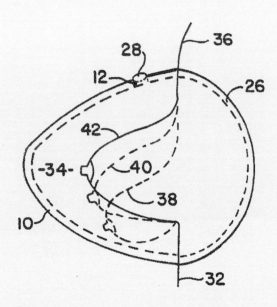

The ultimate in breast control

This watertight bra contains liquid in which the breasts float. The inventor enthuses: "Typically, a breast supported by liquid will yield a shape which appears to be rounded, firm, youthful, and very attractive…" It gets better: "By simply changing liquid pressure, a woman could easily increase or decrease the visible size of her breasts…" The bra cups have been drawn oversize by the illustrator for clarity; however this wonder (why he bothered) bra would only suit women who like being immersed in liquid all day. Yet there's more innovation: "A transparent liquid brassiere is the perfect solution for a woman who wants to display part or all of her breasts while they are invisibly supported into their most flattering shape."

Eating Utensil

Inventor: Gerald L. Printz

Date of patent: March 1989 • Patent number: US Patent 4,809,435

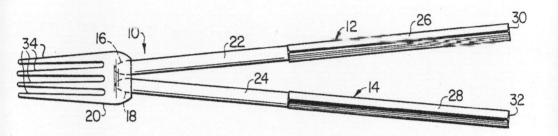

Chop chop

The inventor of this breakthrough in cosmopolitan eating paints a tragic picture of the plight of the Westerner before its arrival: "the use of chopsticks requires a great deal of dexterity, making their use impossible by those without training, and often making their use undesirable by those who do not." This invention will suit those who do not "wish to risk the embarrassment of dropping or otherwise mishandling the food they are eating." But does even the most untrained user need a four-page patent application to understand the principle of this device? Simply fix your chopsticks together and stick a fork on them.

Glove or Mitten Intended to Accommodate Two Hands

Inventor: Terence David King

Date of patent: February 1990 • Patent number: British Patent GB2221607

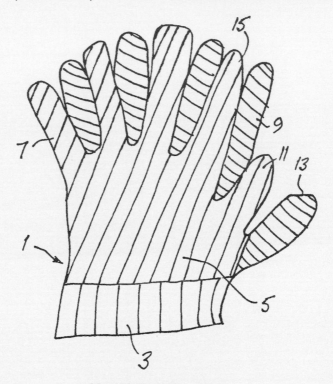

Hand in hand in glove

Who says the British aren't romantic? This double glove—or ten-fingered glove, if you prefer—enables two people to walk hand in hand with their palms in contact, but their fingers warm. Patented on St. Valentine's Day, it would especially suit what the application quaintly calls a "courting couple." The two sections can be made in contrasting colors to give the impression of two conventional gloves. And they can be differently sized, to accommodate a parent and child.

Horseback Transport for the Sick or Injured

Inventor: Hezekiah L. Thistle

Date of patent: January 1837 • Patent number: US Patent 112

Wobbling to safety

If you'd made the mistake of laughing at old Hezekiah's name, you'd probably have ended up in need of his invention: a horse-borne stretcher to get you to hospital quickly. It has its own built-in suspension—the four springs marked (B). You'd certainly get a good view of the countryside up there but the trip might be an ordeal for those prone to seasickness. It would be a hard call as to whether this rock 'n' roll transport was better or worse than being shaken around on a horse-drawn cart or sled.

Insect Destroyer

Inventor: Auguste Le Blanc

Date of patent: May 1870 • Patent number: US Patent 101,028

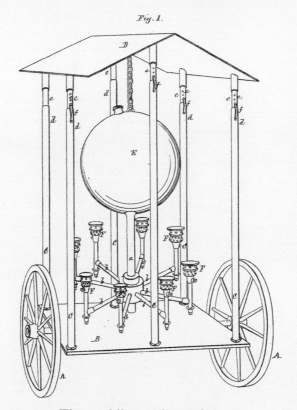

Fig. 1.

The mobile moth-catcher

The cotton fields of the old South were ravaged periodically by the cotton worm. This Louisiana invention was designed to destroy the parent moths before they could reproduce. The cart is wheeled through the cotton field at night. From its roof is suspended a spherical tank, feeding oil or gasoline to the burners hanging beneath. The roof can be raised to make sure the burners are visible over the tallest plants. The doomed moths are attracted by the flames, where most will perish. In a fiendish twist, the underside of the roof is coated with non-drying white paint, which catches moths that have avoided the flames.

Radiation Detector for Cat Flap and 1,000-Megaton Orbital Bomb

Inventor: Arthur Paul Pedrick

Date of patent: March 1976 • Patent number: British Patent GB1426698

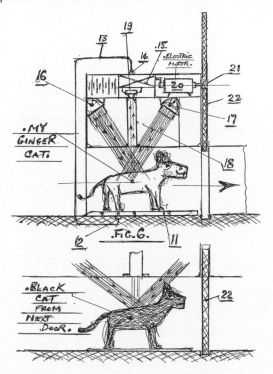

Star wars and intruder moggies

Mr. Pedrick was a former patent examiner who on retirement patented enormous numbers of idiosyncratic devices and processes. It doesn't really matter whether you understand the physics of the diagram as physicists certainly can't. The device is intended to discriminate colors in the light falling on it. Used in an orbital deterrent device, it detects a nuclear attack and retaliates by dropping a colossal bomb on the aggressor country. When controlling a cat-flap it can admit (for example) Mr. Pedrick's pet cat Ginger into the "One-Man Think-Tank Radiation Research Laboratory" (Mr Pedrick's house), while shutting out the pesky black cat from next door.

Thief Trap

Inventor: T. N. Burghart

Date of patent: February 1921 • Patent number: US Patent 1,368,543

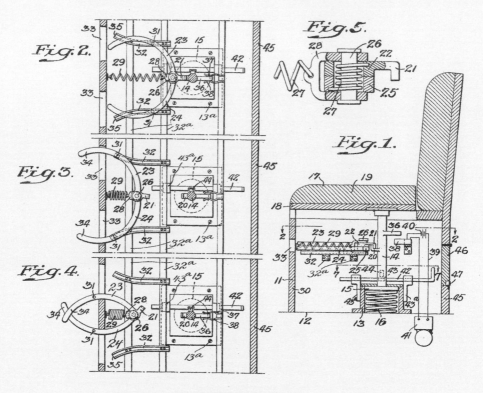

Catch that rider

Stealing cars and joy riding in them isn't a recent fashion; and as far back as 1921 it was thought necessary to take special precautions. This gadget is rather fierce: when the unsuspecting thief sits on the driver's
seat, a telescopic arm shoots out from under the seat and a gripper on the end grabs the thief around
the ankle. (*Figures 2 to 4* show the gripping device in action.) After that a burly policeman or two would
be needed to extract the highly displeased criminal. Of course, the car owner had to be careful to
remember that the device was there.

Apparatus for the Cut of the Mustache

Inventor: Pierre Leon Martin Victor Calmels

Date of patent: June 1927 • Patent number: US Patent 1,633,978

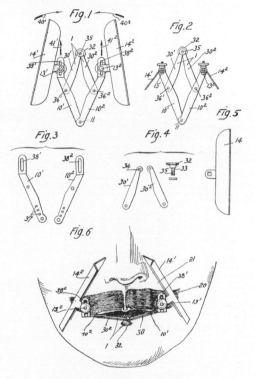

A whiskery wonder

The French nationality of the inventor is reflected in the slightly awry English of the title. How much frustration is hinted at by the application's opening words: "…the least slip of the razor alters the cut. It is then necessary to shorten the mustache indefinitely in order to rectify its line…" Hence this guide device. The swiveling arms *14* (*Fig. 1*) are set to the desired position. The arms *30* and *10*, forming a parallelogram, are gripped in the mouth. Mustache hairs behind and within the bars *14* are spared; those venturing beyond (*20 in Fig. 6*) can safely be lopped off, leaving a perfectly balanced mustache—no need to start whittling in pursuit of symmetry.

Improved Rocking Chair

Inventor: Charles Singer

Date of patent: July 1869 • Patent number: US Patent 92,379

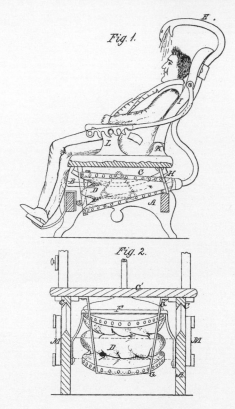

Rock 'n' blow

Some people never want to waste time doing just one thing if they can be doing several at once. This rocking chair operates bellows beneath it, which direct a cooling jet of air over the occupant. Judging by the size of this gentleman's paunch, he might be better advised to try more strenuous exercise. Now if the air-tube were made detachable and flexible, he could also blow on the coals to make the fire hotter, or blow on his soup to make it cooler. What about connecting an accordion to the bellows?

Method of Preserving the Dead

Inventor: Joseph Karwowski

Date of patent: December 1903 • Patent number: US Patent 748,284

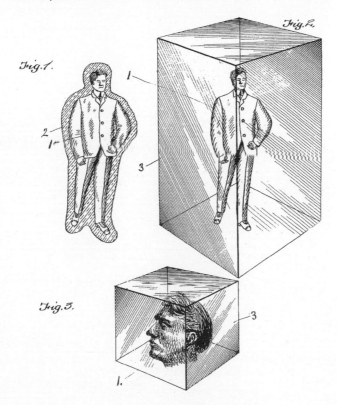

The dear undeparted

All too often, out of sight is out of mind—even for the best-loved of loved ones. Photographs are a mere shadow of the deceased. Wouldn't it be nice if the dead didn't have to depart at all, but could stay right there with us? This process would do the trick. The recently deceased is first covered in a thick layer of water-glass (*Figure 1*). Then a block of molten glass is molded around him or her (*Figure 2*). Being hermetically sealed, with no air able to get in, the body is preserved from decay. Those with less money, or smaller homes, could have the budget option: just the preserved head (*Figure 3*). Surely an interesting talking point in any home...

Apparatus for Developing the Chest

Inventor: Daniel J. Mosher

Date of patent: March 1878 • Patent number: US Patent 201,038

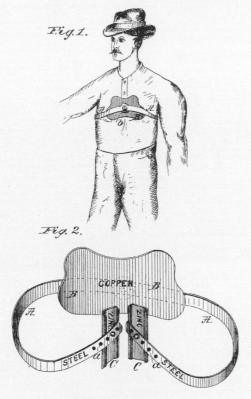

Strong inspiration

The apparatus is put on for short periods several times a day. It consists of a plate of copper (B) and plates of zinc (C) linked by springs of steel that hold the plates tight against the chest and spine. This makes it an effort to breathe and so trains the "muscles of inspiration" (that is, of breathing). The gadget also throws the shoulders forward, forcing the wearer to use his muscles to hold the shoulders back. Copper and zinc have been chosen so that, if the body is moistened, the device acts like a battery and generates a small electric current, "to stimulate the muscles." Clearly Mr. Mosher's device had the spin-off of over-developing the triceps at the same time.

Attachment for Locomotives

Inventor: La Fayette Willson Page

Date of patent: January 1884 • Patent number: US Patent 292,504

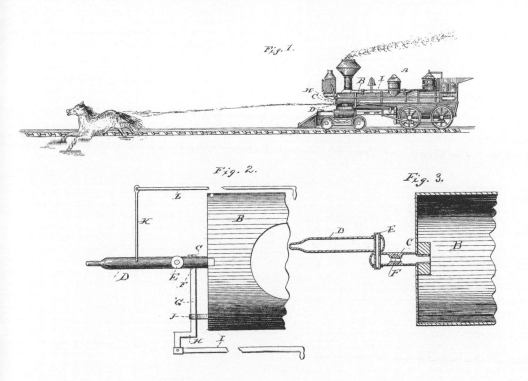

Hose those dogies

Railroad engineers of the old West would much prefer that their cow-catchers never caught a cow, or a wild horse, on the line. The locomotive might well come off as badly as the animal. This device made the loco into a giant water-pistol, capable of clearing the line ahead. A nozzle (D) is mounted on the front of the engine, and when needed, shoots high-pressure water from the boiler. The nozzle can swing from side to side, so that animals round a curve in the line could be shooed off. It's easy to imagine the engineer and fireman squabbling over the right to take a turn on the water gun, and aiming it at quite unsuitable targets along the way. Though you never saw Casey Jones with an Attachment for Locomotives.

Wearable Seating Apparatus

Inventor: Michael Bayley

Date of patent: December 1993 • Patent number: British Patent GB2267208

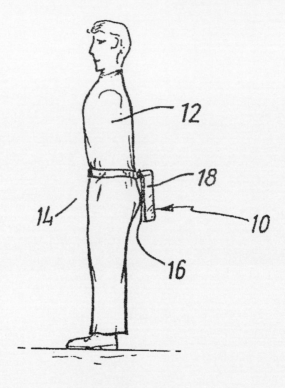

Please be seated

You know that old problem of what to sit on when you're hiking or walking around at an outdoor event: if you carry a cushion or chair with you, you're hopelessly encumbered; if you don't, you find yourself sitting on hard or wet ground, or you give up and stay standing. This invention tackles the problem: wear this cushion on your derriere as you walk around. It'll give you a bonus of extra warmth, so who cares how it looks? Scoffers will laugh on the other sides of their faces when you quickly unsnap a couple of press-studs, and the cushion drops a few inches, held by a restraining strap, perfectly positioned for you to seat yourself on the ground. It may yet become a must-have fashion accessory.

Man-Powered Flying Machine

Inventor: Kuan Shang-Ming

Date of patent: March 1978 • Patent number: US 408,1155

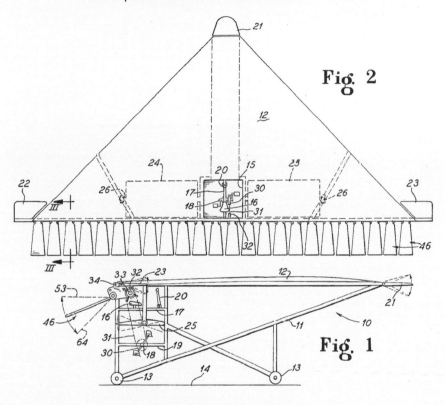

Fig. 2

Fig. 1

Magnificent Flying Machine

The user of this invention will by means of pedal-power "rise from level ground in still air and fly unassisted for a substantial distance," claims the hopeful inventor. By pedaling furiously the pilot rotates a shaft that operates a fan system (consisting of flat fans and elastic bands) mounted at the rear. The fanning of air gives "sufficient propulsive thrust to drive the machine forward." The inventor fails to mention how high the pilot will get or how soft the landing will be. Not recommended for cycling off the tops of cliffs.

Pants Separable at Crotch for Style Mixing

Inventor: Allison Andrews

Date of patent: September 1999 • Patent number: US Patent 6,161,223

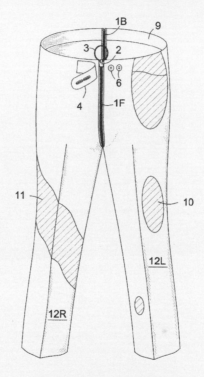

Sartorial psychedelics

Here's a fashion double whammy: mix 'n' match trouser patterns. The left and right sides of these pants are detachable and interchangeable. All you have to do is decide what styles go with which. Separation and recombination are quick and easy, but also secure, so there's no chance of the two halves of today's combination going their separate ways at the wrong moment. And if you happen to rob a bank while wearing this novelty, the witnesses' descriptions will really contradict each other.

Sun-Dial Gravestone

Inventor: Koji Ishidate

Date of patent: September 1997 • Patent number: Japanese Patent JP9256683

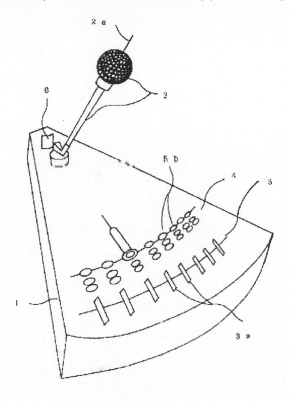

Tomb time

A high-tech tombstone sundial provides reminders of events in the life of the departed. Sunlight is gathered by the concave mirror (6) and reflected to an array of optical fibers. It is channeled along one of these, according to the date and time of day. At the other end of the fiber, the transmitted light is cast onto an engraved clock (3). It also falls on a sequence of markers (4) describing events in the life of the deceased, lighting a lamp at just the right place to give mourners a timely reminder of one of those events. The upright on the sundial can be in a form especially appropriate to the loved one. Here it is a golf putter, but it could equally well be a beer glass, a TV remote, or a donut.

Animal Ear Protectors

Inventor: James D. Williams

Date of patent: November 1980 • Patent number: US Patent 4,233,942

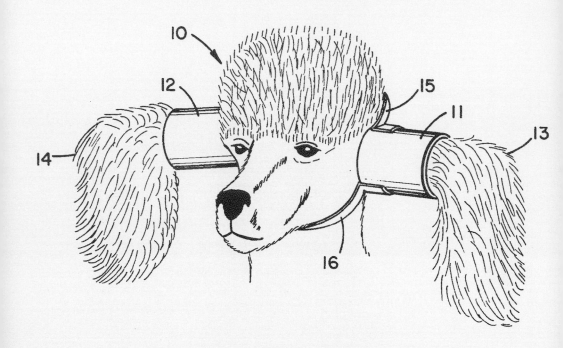

End messy-dog-ear misery

How often have you nuzzled the beautiful long ears of your King Charles spaniel, French poodle, or golden retriever only to find them defiled with dog-meat chunks in gravy? Never? Well, no matter how unobservant you've been, you can be sure your house guests have been laughing at you behind their hands. Lift this shadow from your life now with these simple ear tubes, which sweep your companion animal's ears clear of its meal. As if clean, food-free ears were not enough, this invention "may be itself decorated so as to enhance the appearance of the animal in the eyes of its owner and of others."

Improvement in Coffins

Inventor: Julian A. Fogg

Date of patent: February 1866 • Patent number: US Patent 52,405

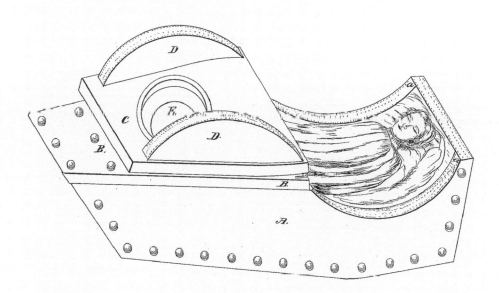

Shown to best advantage

The head portion of this casket is cut away so that mourners can view the deceased even when they are not standing directly alongside the coffin. The lid, seen folded back here, is shaped to fit the lower part of the casket. It contains a viewing window (*E*) for use when closed. Among the advantages described by the inventor is the fact that "many persons can see the corpse without crowding round the coffin." Mr. Fogg was an immigrant from England, where polite people detest that sort of corpse-gazing scrimmage.

Bird Trap Cat Feeder

Inventor: Leo O Voelker

Date of patent: April 1979 • Patent number: US Patent 4,150,505

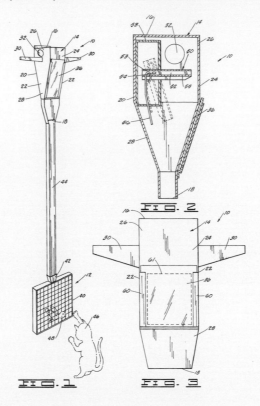

These puny sparrows cannot defeat our superior intellect

A doomed sparrow flies into what seems to be a welcoming birdhouse but is really a diabolically ingenious trap. Inside, it settles on a perch (52), which promptly tips it into the lower part of the "birdhouse." The panic-stricken bird's only way out is down the long tube. At the bottom it finds itself in a cage with a mesh just large enough to poke its head through. Who can blame Mr. Voelker for gloating? "The bird is not able to get the rest of his body through the mesh, but is aided by the cat, who quickly pulls the bird out of the cage with his paw, and is rewarded with a fresh bird dinner."

Hypodermic Syringes and Attachments Thereto Pleasing to Children

Inventor: Robert L Smeton

Date of patent: January 1967 • Patent number: US Patent 3,299,891

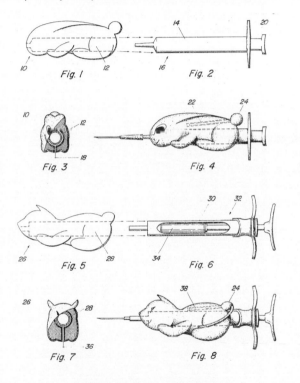

Never trust a bunny

Children are often inclined to be over-fond of rabbits. They overlook their deplorable hygiene and vicious teeth. This invention will change their view of rabbits for life. It consists either of a disposable syringe or a cover for the traditional glass or metal syringe, molded into the shape of a friendly-looking bunny. The young patient—this treatment is not recommended for children not needing an injection—is told in soothing tones that bunny is going to kiss his or her skin, gum or whatever, to help make it better. The painful jab that follows will soon teach them that rabbits are not to be trusted.

Airplane Hijacking Injector

Inventor: Jack Jensen

Date of patent: October 1974 • Patent number: US Patent 3,841,328

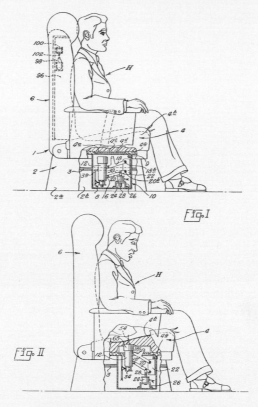

An injection of common sense

In the days when people watched less TV, they were all much more sensitive to each other. People could often tell what a stranger was thinking just by the look in his eyes. This air passenger, for example, was obviously about to hijack the plane. The quick-thinking cabin crew have nipped his plan in the bud by jabbing the schemer in the butt with a hypodermic syringe built into his seat. (All the seats have them—even in business class.) This device may be less useful against the 99.9 percent of hijackers who get out of their seats before revealing themselves. But it could be useful to deal with drunken rowdies or that nun who starts singing hymns when the plane gets engine trouble.

Underwater Breathing Mask

Inventor: Max W. Taylor

Date of patent: August 1949 • Patent number: US Patent 2,477,706

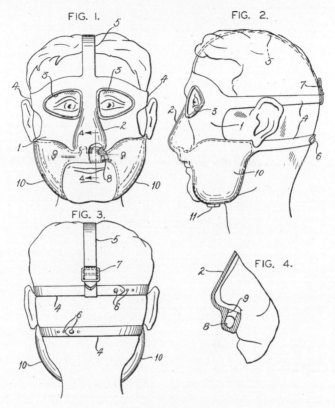

FIG. 1. FIG. 2. FIG. 3. FIG. 4.

In your face

Most kids have dreamed of exploring underwater with just a bagful of air to breathe from. This breathing mask aims to make the dream come true. The mask includes two airbags, one over each cheek, connecting with the nose. The diver takes a lungful of air at the surface through the mouth, and then breathes through the nose underwater. The air from the lungs is breathed repeatedly as it goes in and out of the bags. The inventor explains that the bags hold approximately a lungful of air, which can be rebreathed for approximately a minute and a half before it becomes depleted of oxygen and too rich in carbon dioxide. So you need a good watch as well.

Unicycle Roller Skate

Inventor: Lawrence J. Williamson

Date of patent: April 1979 • Patent number: US Patent 5,106,110

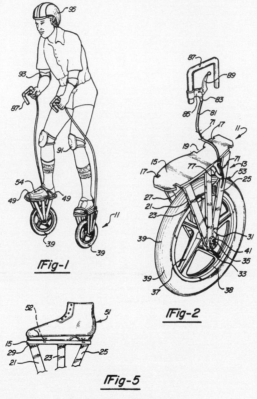

ffig-1

ffig-2

ffig-5

Wheelie impressive

One snag with ordinary roller-skates—traditional or inline—is all those wheels. There are so many to keep maintained, and we're not all skilled mechanics. Admittedly you don't have to put skates up on a jack to change a wheel, but wouldn't it be a lot easier to have just one wheel per foot to think about? Well, here they are: unicycle skates. They even have handbrakes. An emergency stop on one-wheel skates would be pretty spectacular, so the crash helmet is probably essential. Precarious, we hear you say? Pah, get out there and live a little!

Power-Driven Ski

Inventor: Royce H. Husted

Date of patent: June 1976 • Patent number: US Patent 3,964,560

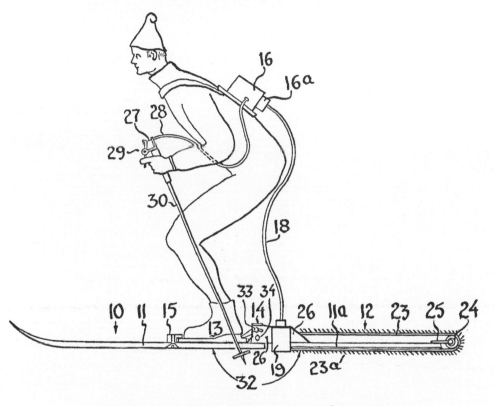

These mountains were too darn quiet, anyway

No more long delays between the thrills of one downhill ski run and the next—now you can have fun skiing uphill and miss out the lines for the ski lifts. And you can start to seriously consider cross-country skiing. All thanks to adding a bit of power to your skis. The engine is a standard gasoline engine for a chain-saw, worn on the back. It drives an endless belt on the back of one or both of your special skis. The belt carries bristles that engage with the snow when the power's on and lie flat for unpowered skiing. Controls are mounted in the handle of your ski pole. Ear plugs will handle the noise problem for the user, if not for everyone else on the slopes.

Bicycle Sail

Inventor: Warren C. Schroeder

Date of patent: April 1984 • Patent number: US Patent 4,441,728

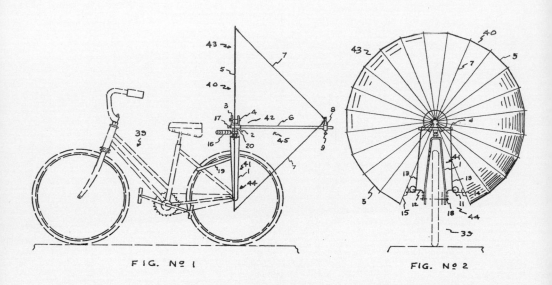

FIG. Nº 1

FIG. Nº 2

Making biking a breeze

Designs for sail-assisted bicycles are legion. Some have towering masts that would put an America's Cup contender to shame. Some have spinnakers mounted for'ard (inventors often resort to nautical lingo in this context). This design is modest by comparison. Forget about beating into the wind, tacking and all that ambitious stuff. Keep the sail furled until the wind is coming from somewhere behind you, then unfold it using the handlebar controls and enjoy the extra thrust. In fact, why not keep it extended when there's no wind? It gives you extra visibility and it's got room for lots of long and hilarious bumper messages.

Amusement Device for a Toilet Bowl or Urinal

Inventor: Louis R. Douglas III

Date of patent: September 1988 • Patent number: US Patent 4,773,863

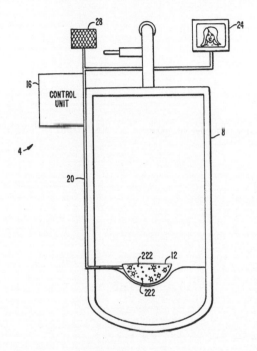

Improving aim: to improve aim

This may be entertainment, but it has high ideals. As the inventor says, it "discourages the inadvertent or intentional diversion of urine outside the proper receptacle. Urine is detected by pressure or temperature sensors, sending an electrical signal to a control unit. This activates a loudspeaker and video screen, to provide audio and visual signals. The combination of sight and sound may be varied by the user upon proper direction of the urine stream, and the user is actively involved in his own amusement." But we who detest rest-room TV—where shall we direct our urine streams?

Amphibious Single Horse-Drawn Light Vehicle

Inventor: Jude Bernard

Date of patent: February 1994 • Patent number: French Patent FR2694256

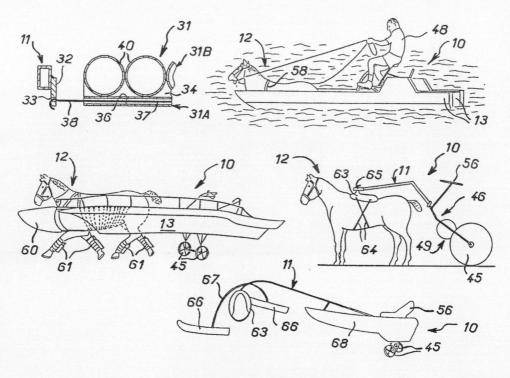

You can take a horse to water...

The inventor has attached two long floats to the shafts of a sulky, or single-seat carriage. There are wheels at the front of the floats and the driver has pedals driving the carriage wheels to help the vehicle get around on land. The rear wheels can be in the form of additional floats. Pedaling in the water could help, too, if paddles are attached to the back wheels. So why would you want to build an amphibious horse-drawn vehicle? One option, says the inventor, is to compete in horse water sport. What horse water sport? We need to invent one. Could be an idea for a patent there.

Limb Movement Exercising and Training Apparatus

Inventor: Kenneth W. Hundley

Date of patent: September 1993 • Patent number: US Patent 5,242,344

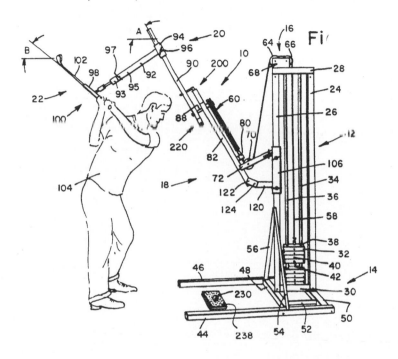

It don't mean a thing if it ain't got that swing

Is there a better way to practice your golf swing than to just go out on the course and play golf? Heck, there has to be, or else the American patent golf exerciser industry will grind to a halt. This apparatus aims to combine weight training with exercising strokes in golf or an unlimited number of sports, such as tennis, baseball, swimming, or martial arts. But will you get the best of both worlds, or the worst? After a few weeks' hard work with this machine, you might find that you've got the build of Arnie Schwarzenegger on one side and that you have to tie lead weights on your golf club to make it feel right.

Night Light for a Toilet

Inventor: Brooke B. Pattee

Date of patent: November 1993 • Patent number: US Patent 5,263,209

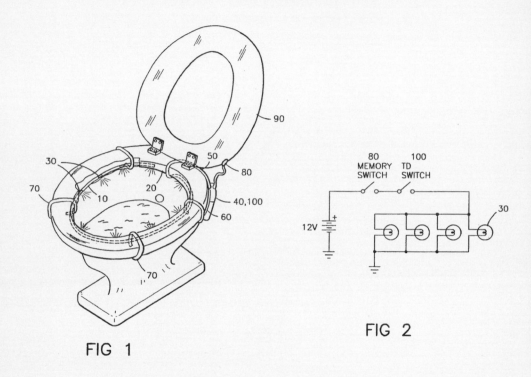

FIG 1

FIG 2

Let the light shine on you

When nature inconsiderately calls in the small hours and you struggle to the bathroom, trauma may await: "To one whose eyes are dark-adapted, switching on a bathroom light can be a painful, temporarily blinding experience that can last several minutes," says the inventor, and people "whose eyes are dark-adapted, therefore are usually faced with the unpleasant choice of using the bathroom with either too little light or with too much light." But now this bathroom enhancement can guide you. The light is provided by lamps in a transparent cable around the inside of the rim. However, nothing in this life is perfect: one day you're going to have to face the icky task of changing a lightbulb.

Life Preserver and Swimming Machine

Inventors: O. B. Lyon and W. H. Young

Date of patent: May 1910 • Patent number: US Patent 957,513

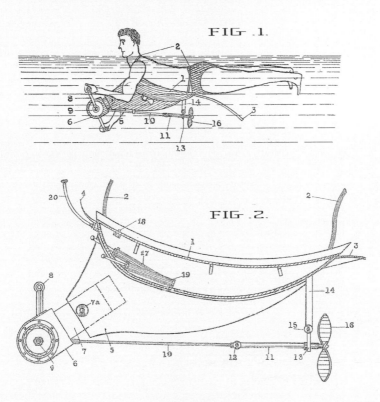

FIG .1.

FIG .2.

Floating on air

Wouldn't you want one of these if your ship had gone down? This device incorporates an air-tight compartment (*1*) to keep the wearer afloat and a hand-operated propeller (*16*) to get him to that rescue ship that would otherwise be just a little too far away. Straps at the neck and waist hold the apparatus on. The hand-cranks and propeller are mounted on a keel made in two parts (*5, 6*) to make it fully adjustable. Air can be released from the air-container and water can be admitted, if necessary, to adjust its buoyancy.

Scalp-Cooling Device

Inventor: Blanche B. Cole

Date of patent: December 1938 • Patent number: US Patent 2,139,001

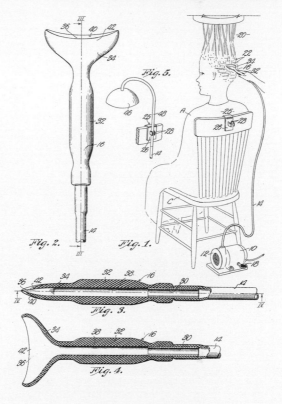

Keeping a cool head

Back in '38 Ms Cole found another one of those terrors from which inventors perpetually battle to defend us: in a hair salon, "steam sometimes escapes from permanent-wave heaters and causes a burning to the scalp therebeneath." So when the smell of cooking pervades the beauty parlor, the present cooling device comes into play, "whereby the cool air may be quickly and definitely directed to the overheated portion of the scalp to immediately relieve the overheated condition." But in today's litigious world, wouldn't the cooked and chilled client already be calling her lawyer?

Spherical Rolling-Hull Marine Vessel

Inventor: Alessandro O. Dandini

Date of patent: January 1976 • Patent number: US Patent 3,933,115

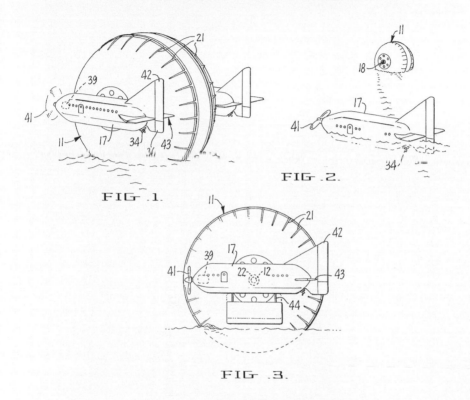

FIG. 1.

FIG. 2.

FIG. 3.

In the proud tradition of the *Titanic*

This globular ship is rotated by motors inside the ball. When rolling, its motion causes it to rise out of the water, reducing drag. The vessel is helped along and steered by propellers and rudders on the cabins at each side of the sphere. Cargo is carried within the sphere, and both within and beneath the cabins. If the crew in a side cabin detect an emergency, or suffer a sudden loss of faith in the invention, they can fire explosive bolts, detach the cabin and sail on as an independent vessel. That leaves the sphere to be rolled over by the unbalanced weight of the other cabin, whose crew will be wishing they'd separated first.

Improved Burglar Trap

Inventor: William Carr

Date of patent: May 1868 • Patent number: US Patent 77,582

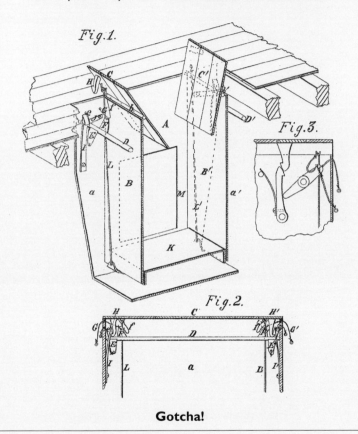

Fig.1.

Fig.3.

Fig.2.

Gotcha!

Troubled by burglars? When you lock up the store at night, just set this neat trap for them. An unsuspecting intruder who steps on the trap doors will go straight through into the chamber below. Landing on the floor, his weight will pull the doors firmly to, locking them by the catches. The following morning you can pull out a disgruntled miscreant. Or, if you return after a two-week vacation, you can pull out the cold, lifeless body. Oh, and remember to tell the cleaner you've installed it.

Mustache-Guard for Cups

Inventor: Edwin H. Green

Date of patent: October 1898 • Patent number: US Patent 29,466

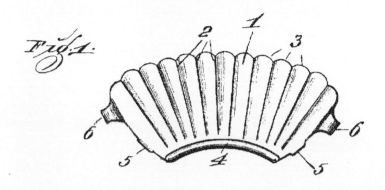

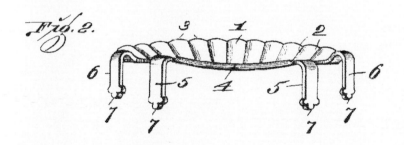

Mustaches and tea shouldn't mix

The cultivation, care, and appreciation of mustaches was a major industry throughout much of the nineteenth century. (Is it a mere coincidence that the mustache's fall from favor after World War I was soon followed by the Great Depression?) One flourishing trade within this industry was the design of mustache-guards for cups. In this design the tongues (5) grip the cup. The guard covers most of the top of the cup, allowing the welcome beverage to flow out, but preventing the mustache from intruding. The elegant scalloping of the guard's top surface not only delights the eye but—who knows?—may well have gently combed the mustache.

Interpersonal-Introduction Signaling System

Inventor: Carlisle H. Dickson

Date of patent: October 1979 • Patent number: US Patent 4,173,016

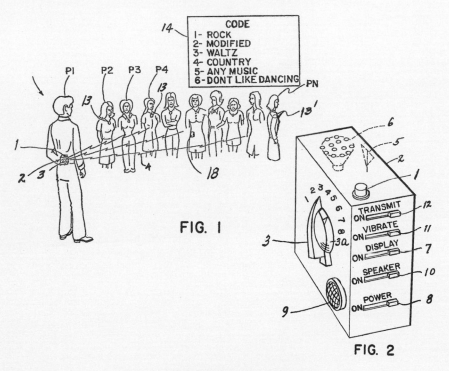

CODE
1- ROCK
2- MODIFIED
3- WALTZ
4- COUNTRY
5- ANY MUSIC
6- DONT LIKE DANCING

FIG. 1

TRANSMIT ON
VIBRATE ON
DISPLAY ON
SPEAKER ON
POWER ON

FIG. 2

Saturday night bleeper

Cellphone technology still hasn't caught up with this 1979 vision. Although today it's beautifully simple to call someone you know, how do you contact the person you want to get to know? The hopeful young dude on the left is broadcasting coded signals from a transmitter as discreetly compact as 1979 technology would permit. The signal represents one of a small number of preset messages. Suitably equipped ladies receive the signal, and if they wish can send a signal back. If they're wearing the appropriate necklaces (*13*), lights on them can flash. "The parties can then advance and meet," says the inventor. But what happens when fifteen guys turn up with the same device...?

Facial Muscles Exercise Mask

Inventor: Johnathan G. Crawford

Date of patent: May 1987 • Patent number: US Patent 4,666,148

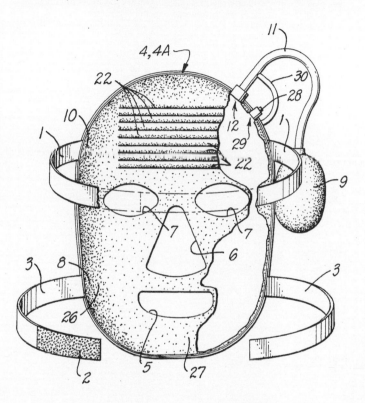

You'll look beautiful when you take this off

Cares and years may have left their mark on your features, but you can fight back with this pneumatic aid. The plastic mask is held over your face by headbands. Inside it has an inflatable lining that you can pump up with the hand-pump shown, getting a little useful hand exercise in the process. Then run through your normal facial exercise routine, but now working against increased resistance. Above the eye sockets, an air-pressure gauge and a timer have been mounted to display either time elapsed or estimated calories consumed. Just be careful to shout a warning to anyone entering the room, or you'll have a heart-attack victim to deal with.

Communicating Device for Human Beings and Animals

Inventor: Karola Baumann; Adrian De Kaart; William Hodali

Date of patent: May 1998 • Patent number: German Patent WO98/21939

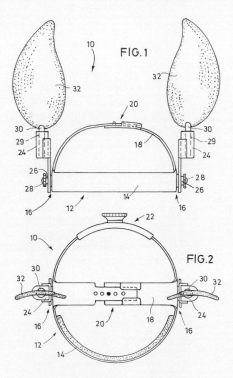

Prick up your ears

Animals often have such expressive ears. Think of the busily twitching, rotating, flapping, flattening ears of dogs, cats, horses, or elephants. Humans, in contrast, sometimes waggle their ears for a party trick, but never hold long conversations by this means. Hence we miss the chance to communicate with our animal friends. That is why these three inventors have pooled their talents to create these mobile ears, which can be independently set at any of a vast range of angles. The inventors report that they have communicated successfully with horses using such ears. What the horses said is confidential, but perhaps it was on the lines of, "Hey, guys, you should really patent those!"

Floater Waterbed

Inventor: Peter W. Silberling

Date of patent: May 1987 • Patent number: US Patent 4,662,010

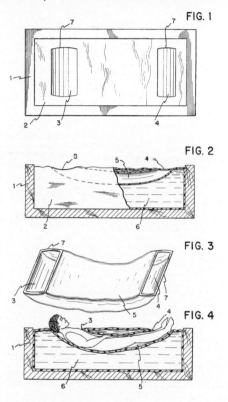

FIG. 1

FIG. 2

FIG. 3

FIG. 4

Floating to nirvana

Waterbeds are often associated with certain vigorous activities, the very opposite of restful. But this adaptation will float you peacefully away from the everyday world of day-to-day cares. A sort of pocket is built into the waterbed, a "free-floating sleeve," in which you can lie, enjoying the buoyancy of the water, while staying warm and dry. There is no mention of a heater for the water in the bed and perhaps one will be needed on those winter mornings when you most want to enjoy a lie-in, that's if you don't want to feel like Ernest Shackleton, adrift on the ice pack.

Alarm Fork

Inventors: Nicole M. Dubus; Susan Springfield

Date of patent: June 1995 • Patent number: US Patent 5,421,089

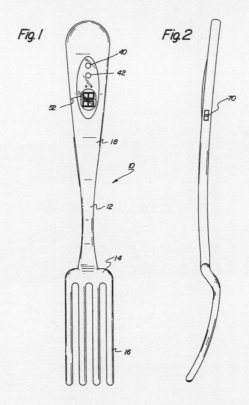

Not tactful for guests

There are countless existing designs of fork, concedes the patent application, but they share a disadvantage: none of them has a built-in timer giving the eater permission to take the next bite. This crying need is now met. A red light flashes on the handle until a preset time has passed. The light turns green, you grab another mouthful, and the countdown starts again. The fork can beep too, if you want it to. You certainly won't rush through your meals with this little gadget around. After a while you may even stop looking forward to them.

Knee Vanity

Inventor: Jack E. Alexander

Date of patent: April 1961 • Patent number: US Patent 2,979,990

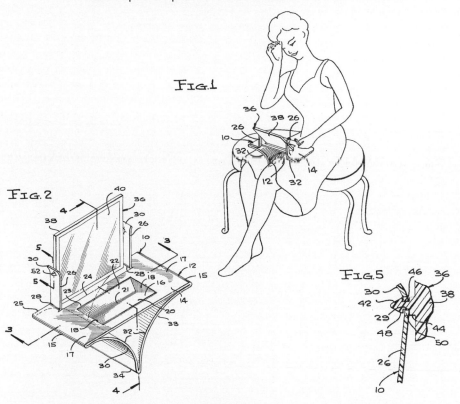

Vanity, vanity …

What is a knee vanity? No, it's not the vice of pride with regard to one's own knees. It is this miniature dressing-table that, as the inventor explains, can "be clampably engaged between the knees." It has a detachable mirror, in front of which is a recess to hold toilet articles. It is especially useful when traveling by train, car, or plane when "a full-size mirror, vanity table, or other accessories may not be available." (And that's certainly a real problem. When did you last have access to a full-size vanity table while flying? On your last Zeppelin trip?)

Urinal for use by Females

Inventor: Kathleen K. Jones

Date of patent: August 1987 • Patent number: US Patent 4,683,598

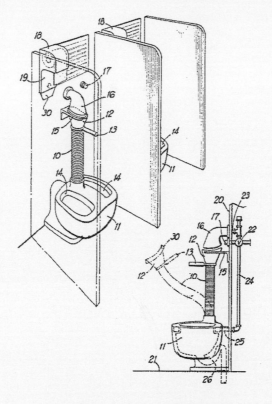

Will women stand for it?

With women successfully challenging men in so many areas, technology is now poised to help them storm another male bastion: standing urination. We'll let the inventor's own words take us through this delicate area: "Specifically, this invention discloses a urinal which can be utilized by females while in a generally upright position and may be advantageously used in public restrooms and the like." Trouble is, after an evening hitting the happy juice, a woman—like a man—may have trouble maintaining a generally upright position and may be hoping for a nice restful sit-down in the restroom.

Beauty Device

Inventor: Richard J. Shebib

Date of patent: September 1964 • Patent number: US Patent 3,148,386

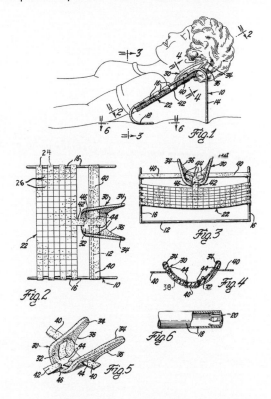

Ideal for the stationary sleeper

Before this invention came on the scene the price of tonight's wonderful deep sleep was tomorrow's bad hair day. "It is a particular problem with women having recently arranged hairdos or coiffures to find a way to sleep or recline without destroying much of the beauty that attends freshly done hair," intones the inventor. So this device consists of a "flexible or webbed surface" to support the shoulders and "a pair of finger-like members extending upwardly therefrom to engage and support the skull." But it looks as if you would need to exercise iron self-control—everything would be spoiled if you were to roll onto your side in your sleep.

Amphibious Bicycle

Inventor: Takei Toshitaka

Date of patent: January 1999 • Patent number: Japan Patent JP11011124

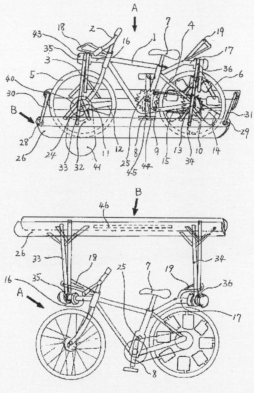

Cycling frenzy

The Bible says that Jesus could walk on water, but with this invention you could "ride" on it. The amphibious bicycle is supported by floats attached to struts which project from the main frame. In normal use, when the rider doesn't fancy crossing a river or harbor, the struts fold up and above the bike and out of the way—as long as the rider is very short or doesn't mind crouching. How this would affect the aerodynamic capabilities of the bike is anyone's guess, but it saves fiddling about adding lots of extra floats whenever the desire to plunge into a lake takes the cycler's fancy.

Secure Pants

Inventor: Ta Baozu

Date of patent: October 2000 • Patent number: Chinese Patent WO 01/78536

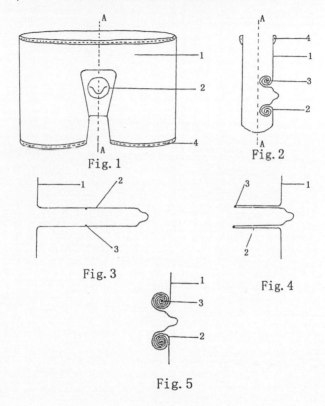

Fig. 1

Fig. 2

Fig. 3

Fig. 4

Fig. 5

Pants protection

This invention takes the idea of "all in ones" to the extreme. No need for men to worry about sexually transmitted disease any longer, as the Secure Pants act as a form of contraception too. They will seal a man's lower half safely and neatly with a combination of plastics and rubber that expand and contract as the need arises. Presumably it can only be worn once, but perhaps it's best not to dwell on the details.

Chocolate Sausage Snack

Inventor: Francisco Molina Ucles

Date of patent: October 2003 • Patent number: Spanish Patent WO 03/084353

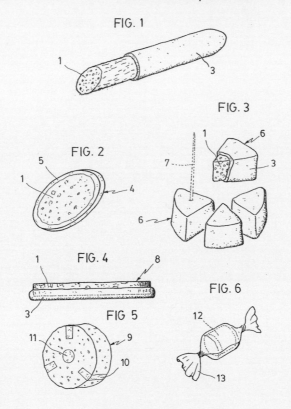

Sweet and sour

Not too hard to resist, this snack does not require "any type of heat treatment or culinary manipulation," according to its description. Apart from this small advantage, the chocolate sausage snack's odd combination of ingredients promises a unique taste experience to say the least. The meat consists of sausages "without the casing" and the chocolate of any type "used for frostings in pastry," which is then shaped into bars, slices, or portions. Most people leave the coffee creams to fester at the bottom of the chocolate box, but perhaps here is another candidate to join the ranks of least favorite chocolate centers.

Apparatus for Simulating a "High Five"

Inventor: Albert Cohen

Date of patent: December 1993 • Patent number: US 5,356,330

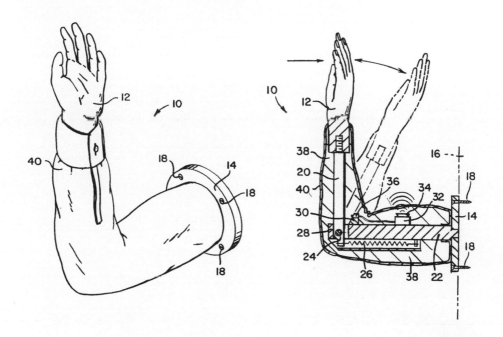

Gimme five

Ever been home alone watching the game on television but had no-one to celebrate with when your team scores? Well here's the answer: an arm that simulates a "high five" slap when the user hits against it. "During a televised sporting event, a 'high five' is commonly shared between fans to express the joy and excitement of a touchdown, home run, game-winning basket, birdie or other positive occurrence," explains the inventor. The "solitary fan" can't perform this ritual, so he came up with a solution—an artificial arm that's just like the real thing. "The arm can be made with any style of hand and may also include sounds." Two other big advantages: You don't have to buy it beer and it always agrees with you.

Improvement in Horizontal Windmills

Inventor: John M. Van Osdel

Date of patent: March 1841 • Patent number: US Patent US 2,003

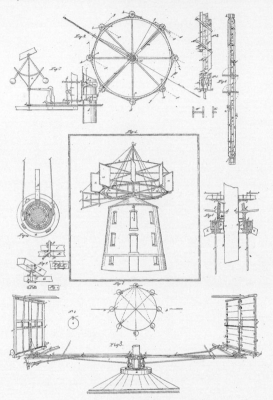

Tilted Windmill

There was obviously enough of a need for improved windmills in 1841 to prompt Mr. Van Osdel to pen this patent, but it does raise the question of why having a wind-wheel perched on top of the building is a better design. In all other aspects it appears to be more or less the same as a conventional windmill, but its much more precarious nature may explain why it never came into existence. It does have one advantage, however, unlike those in Cervantes' classic in which the confused Don Quixote jousts with a windmill he mistakes for an ogre, he would never have reached the sails on this one.